Alaska DOODLES

SASQUATCH BOOKS
SEATTLE

Illustrated and Written by John Skewes

Manufactured in the United States of America by Malloy Incorporated,
(Michigan) in February 2011
Published by Sasquatch Books
Distributed by PGW/Perseus

17 16 15 14 13 12 11   9 8 7 6 5 4 3 2 1

Book design by Sarah Plein

Library of Congress Cataloging-in-Publication data is available.

ISBN-10: 1-57061-727-9
ISBN-13: 978-1-57061-727-0

Sasquatch Books
119 South Main Street, Suite 400
Seattle, WA 98104
(206) 467-4300
www.sasquatchbooks.com
custserv@sasquatchbooks.com

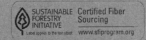

THE PANHANDLE

This is Debbie and Danny.
What does Alaska make them think of?

What did Debbie pack?

What did Danny pack?

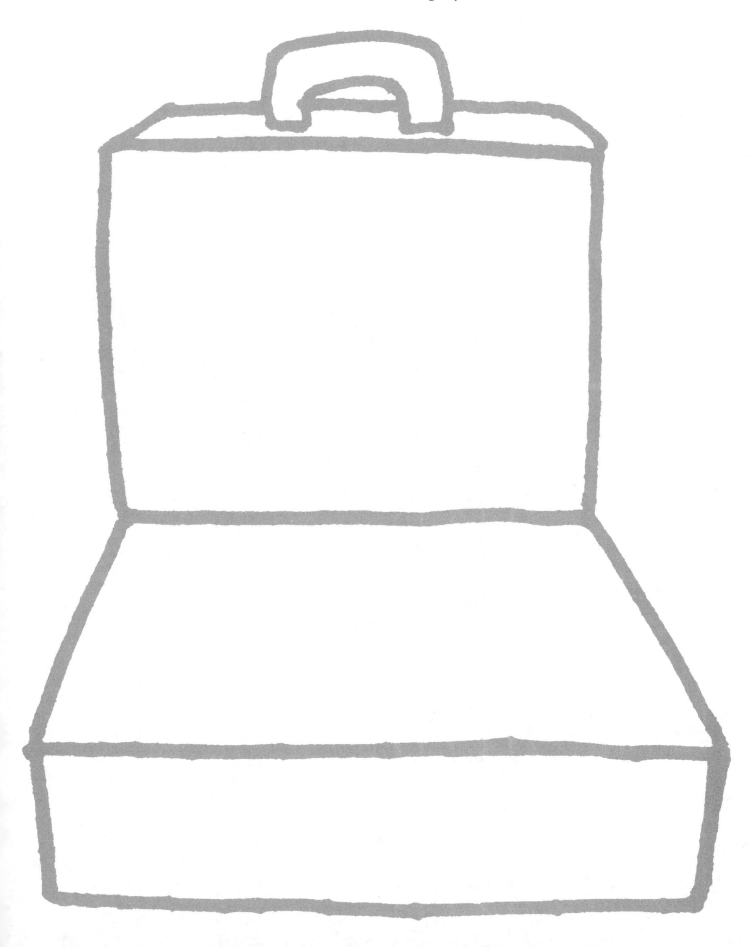

There are no roads to Juneau!
How will you get there?

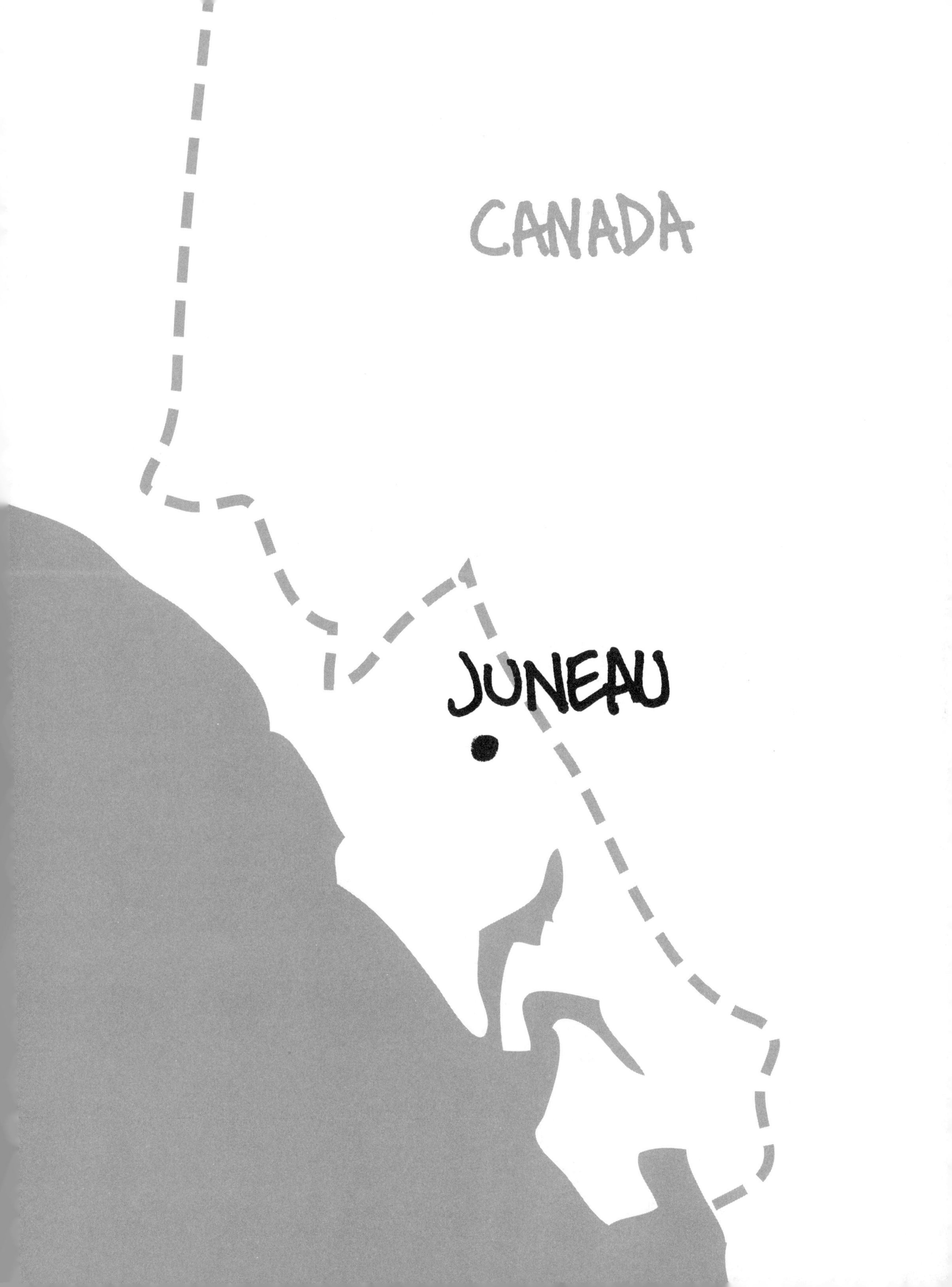
CANADA
JUNEAU

Find the words: glacier, Juneau, Sitka, Skagway, totem.

```
R A A Q Y U S
H E P V A Y I
N X I E W F T
V V N C G D K
C U R Z A S A
J N M W K L N
Z Q A L S F G
T O T E M B M
```

Draw quills on the porcupine.

Draw people on the cruise ship.

It's very foggy. What's in the fog?

Draw a lighthouse for the ship.

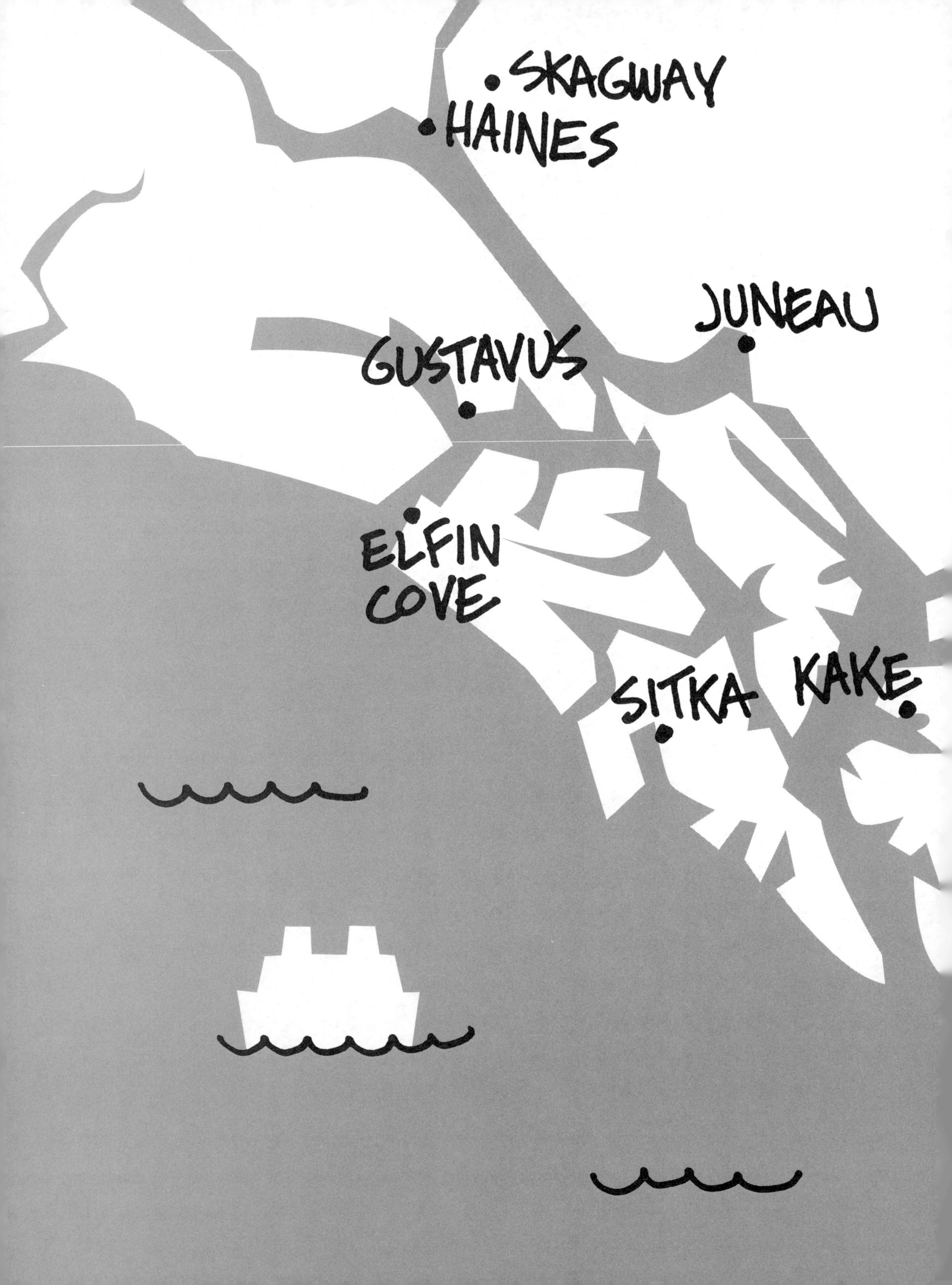
SKAGWAY
HAINES
JUNEAU
GUSTAVUS
ELFIN COVE
SITKA
KAKE

Navigate your ship to all the ports
of the Inside Passage.

PETERSBURG

WRANGELL

.KETCHIKAN

.CRAIG

PRINCE
RUPERT.

Oh no! Mosquitoes!

Color the flags on the cruise ship.

Ketchikan

Color the totem poles.

Now make your own totem poles.

Draw a big glacier.

Glacier Bay

What do they see?

Give them sunglasses.

Uh-oh. Draw a mosquito biting you.

Now swat him!

Draw more salmonberries for
Debbie and Danny to eat.

Who else is eating them?

Draw mud puddles for them to jump in.

Color the mask.

Tlingit mask

Now make your own.

.

Hang some salmon from the rack to dry.

Crossword

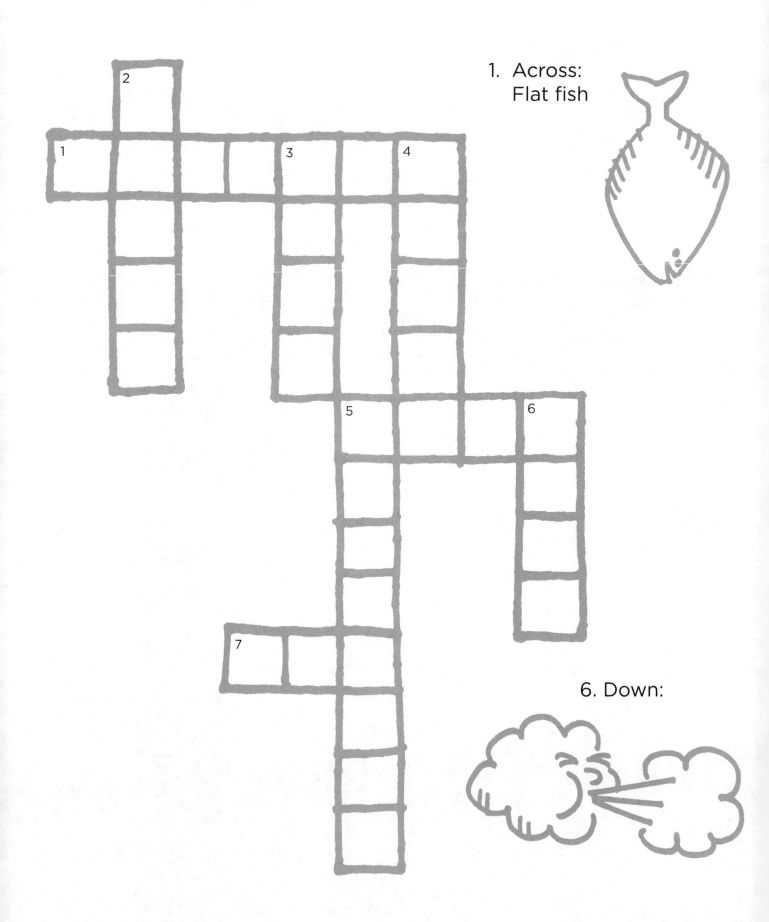

1. Across:
   Flat fish

6. Down:

2. Down:

3. Down:

4. Down:

5. Across:

5. Down (2 words):

7. Across:

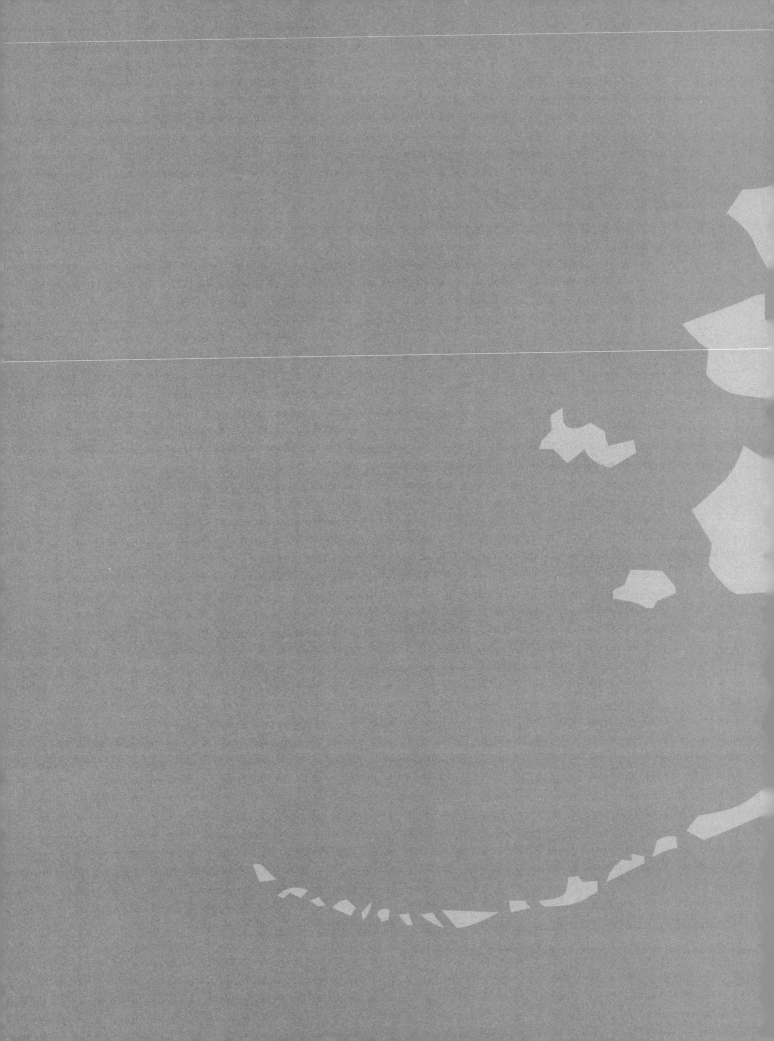

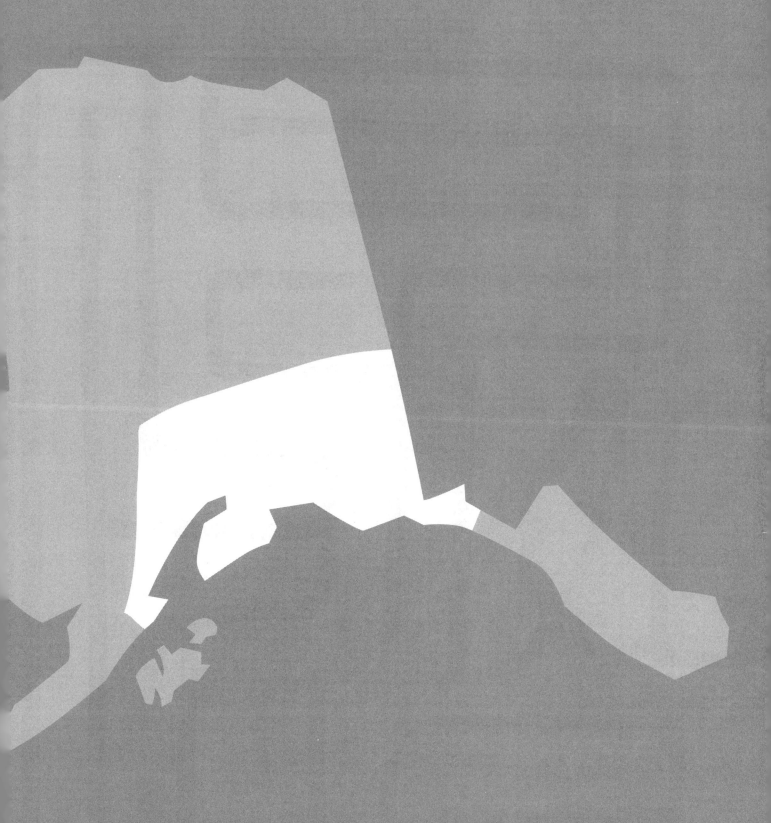

SOUTH CENTRAL

Follow the leash to find Larry.

How many fish can you
catch in your net?

Giant vegetables grow in Alaska because of the long summer days.

Draw a giant pumpkin.

Draw a giant cabbage.

Find the words: bear, eagle, halibut, Homer, snow.

```
X X V Q D W T
H O M E R U B
E E C J B M E
M Z A I R S A
X J L G N B R
G A W O L Q S
H Z W V M E C
X K Z C O H X
```

Draw wolf cubs in the den.

People wear crazy fur hats at the
Fur Rendezvous ("Fur Rondy") Festival.

Connect the dots.

Draw birds on the pilings.

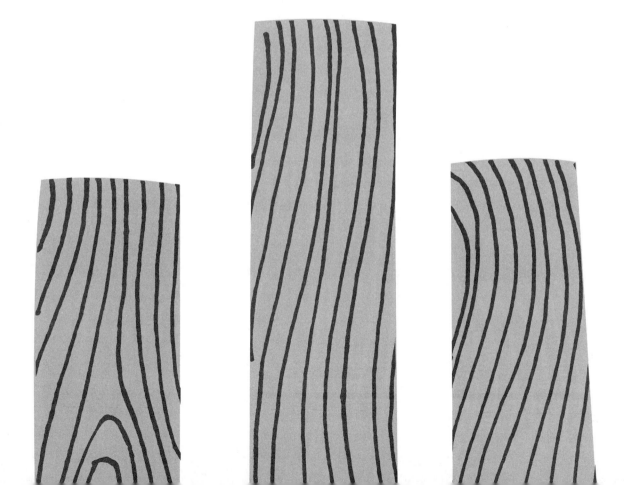

What did you catch?

Draw someone to get the
puck past the goalie.

Decorate the snowman.

Help Pete find his dog Larry.

How many snowballs can you make?

How far can Danny throw
the moose dropping?

What can you make out of the moose dropping?

Moose Dropping Festival, Talkeetna

Draw the tracks of the ice-skater.

How far has the lumberjack chopped the tree?

Now draw a big fire to get warm.

Where will the snowmobile go?

Ride a snowmobile uphill.

Ride a sled downhill.

What's in the surf?

What's on the shore?

What is under the water?

What is floating on the water?

What is flying over the water?

Draw the rain.

Is it snowing or raining?

...or both?

Snowball fight!!!

Draw sails on the old sailing ship.

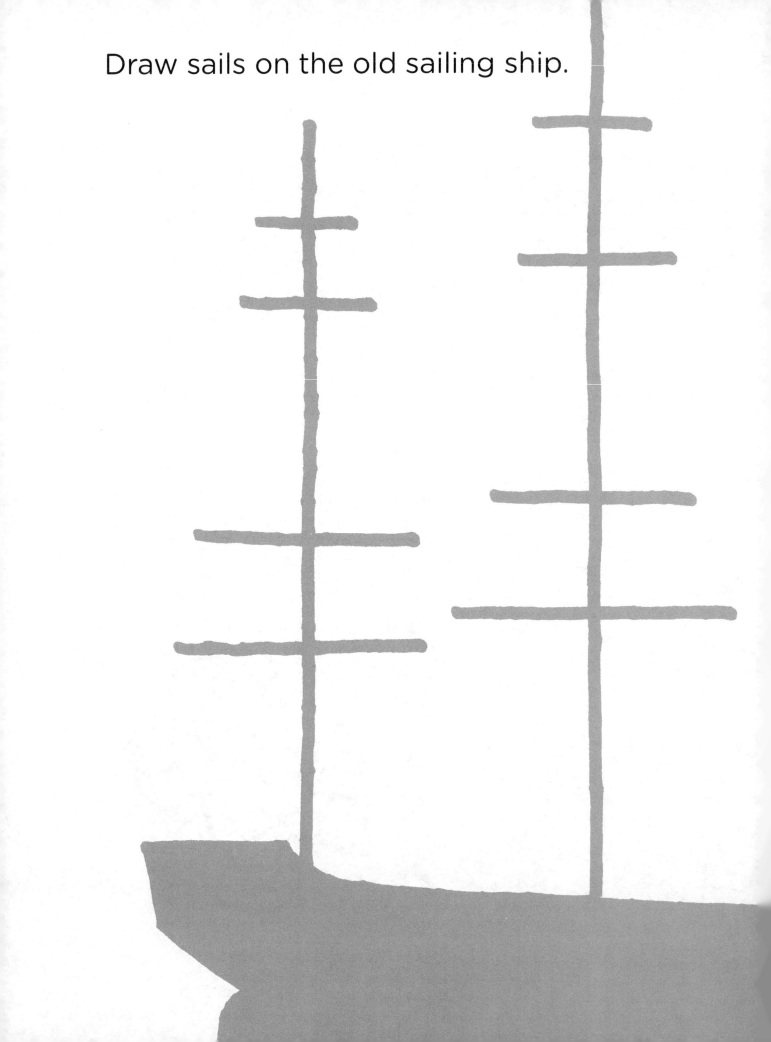

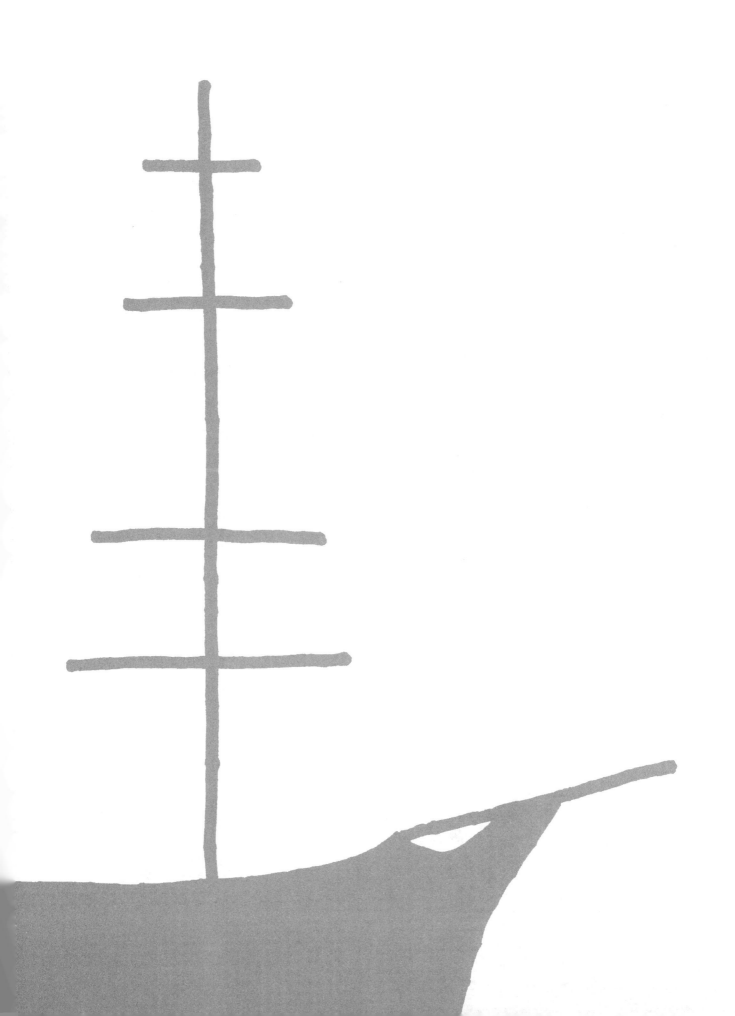

Draw a Coast Guard helicopter to rescue the boater.

SOUTH WEST

Alaska is the biggest state.
Draw something BIGGER than Alaska.

What did the sea lion eat?

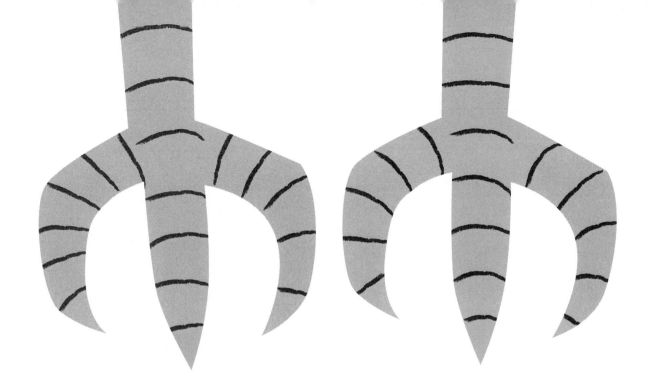

What did the eagle catch in its claws?

Color the king crab.

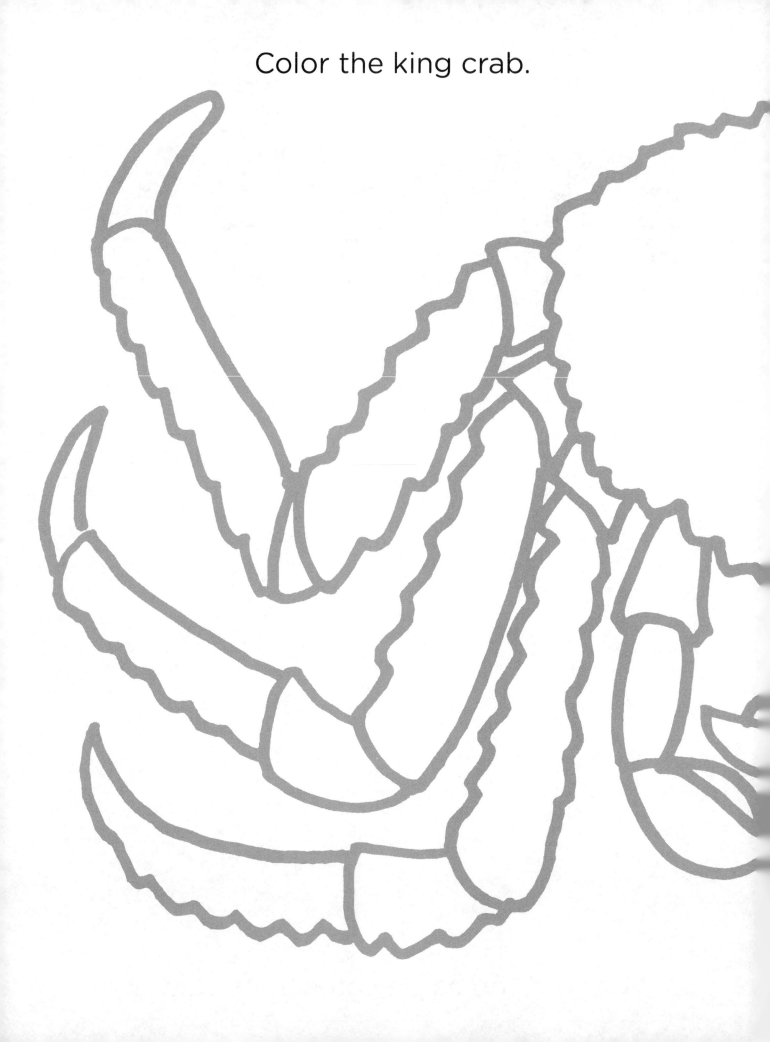

A volcano is erupting!

Mount Shishaldin, Aleutian Islands

Which way is southwest on the compass?

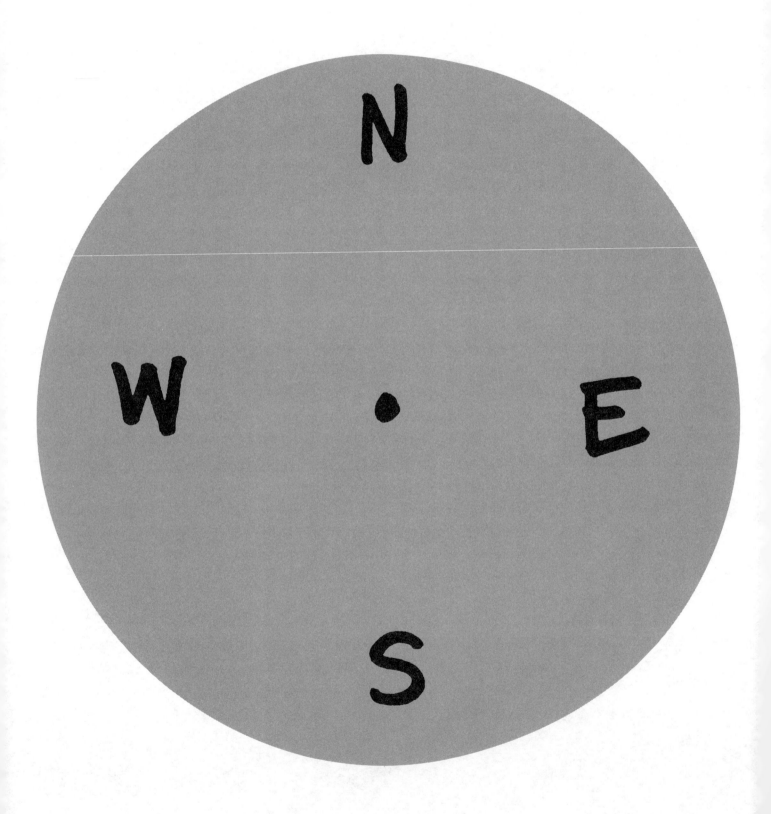

Which way do you want to go?

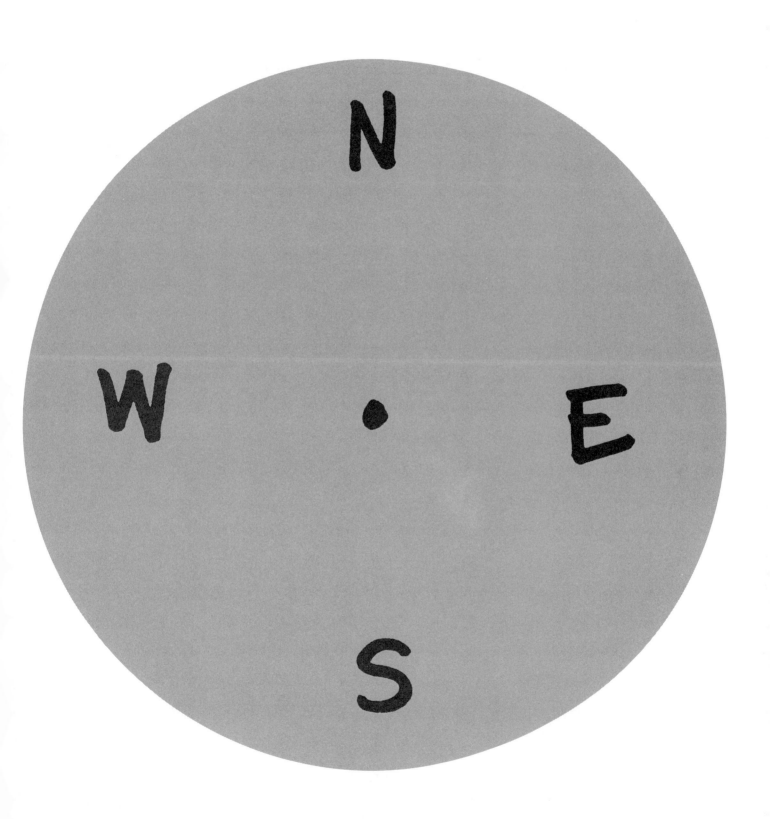

Find the words: kayak, Kodiak, salmon, volcano, whale.

```
K V E L W K T
A O F L O Q C
Y L U D A B H
A C I Q R H Z
K A T S Q Z W
K N O M L A S
L O V X X B D
Q O L D M X D
```

Draw hot water shooting
from the geyser.

Umnak Island

Draw the baby eagle hatching.

What is the sea otter eating?

Help the kayak get through the ice.

Who is being tossed in the blanket toss?

Draw spots on the lynx.

This is a whale's tail.
Draw the rest of the whale.

Draw an eagle in the tree.

Draw a salmon for the eagle to catch.

Can the fish escape the net?

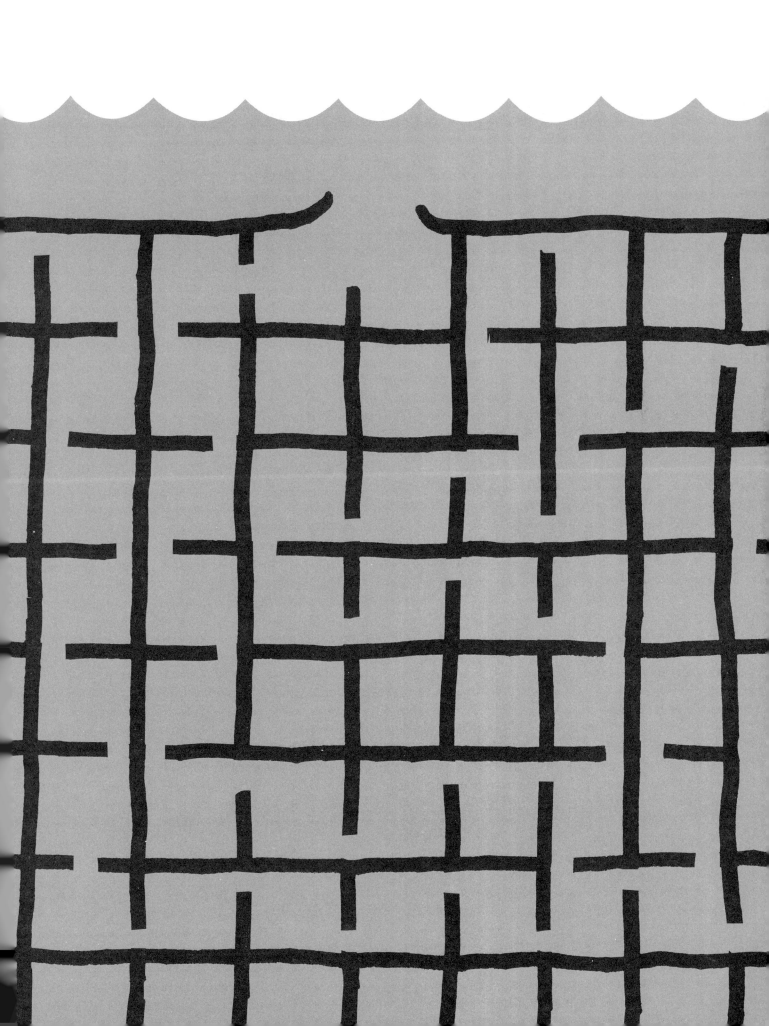

What is the bear chasing?

What is chasing the bear?

Does this plane have
wheels, floats, or skis?

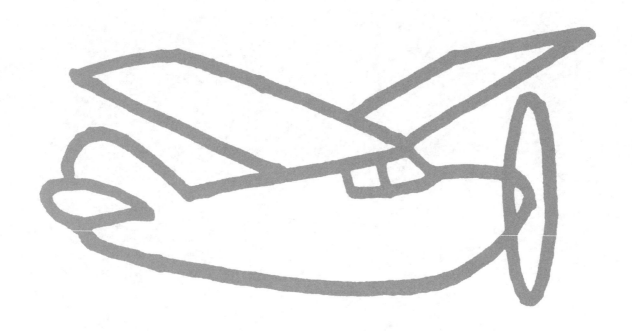

Quick! Draw a place for it to land.

Draw the salmon jumping upstream.

Did the bear catch one?

What did the fisherman catch?

How many fishing boats
are tied to the dock?

Which are black bears, which are brown bears, and which are polar bears?

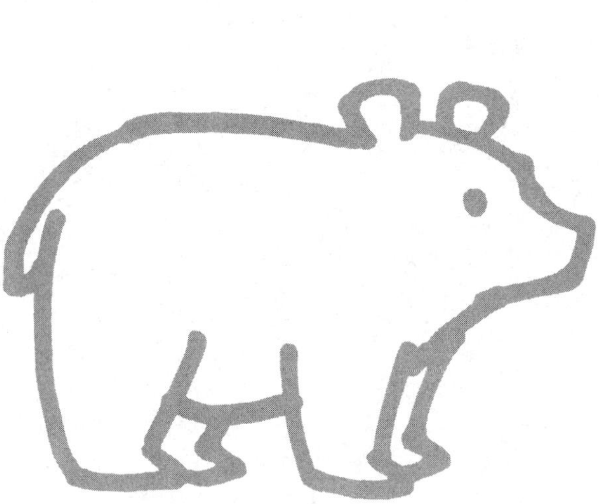
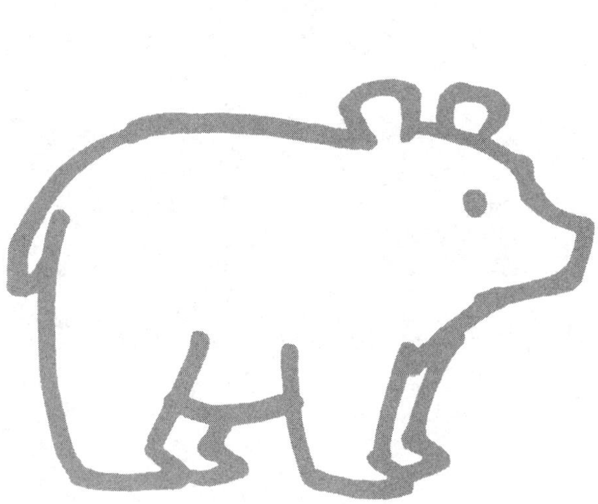
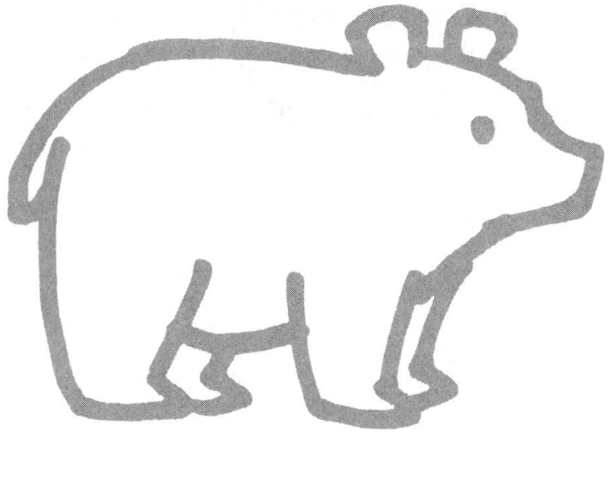
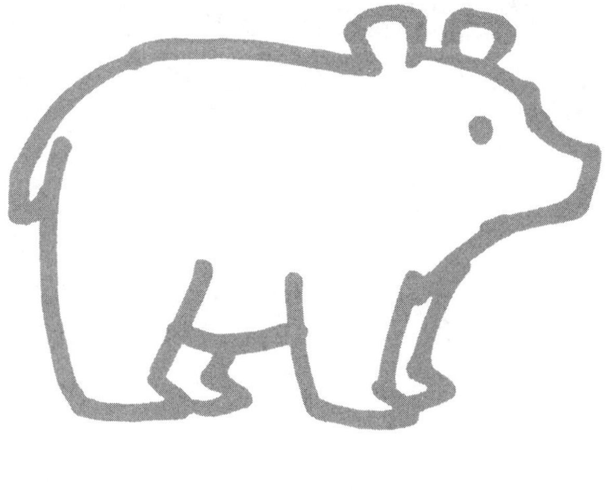
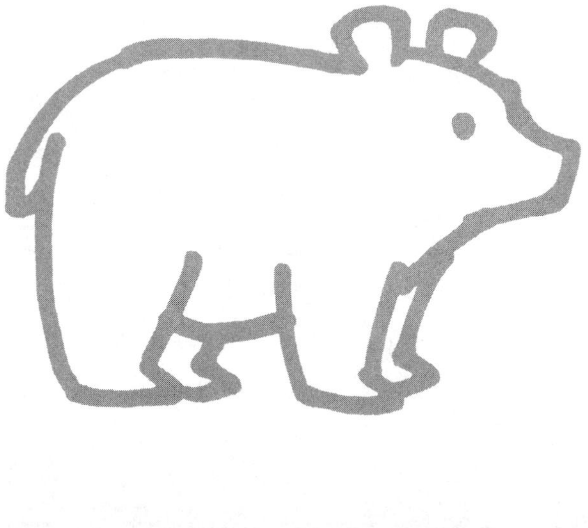
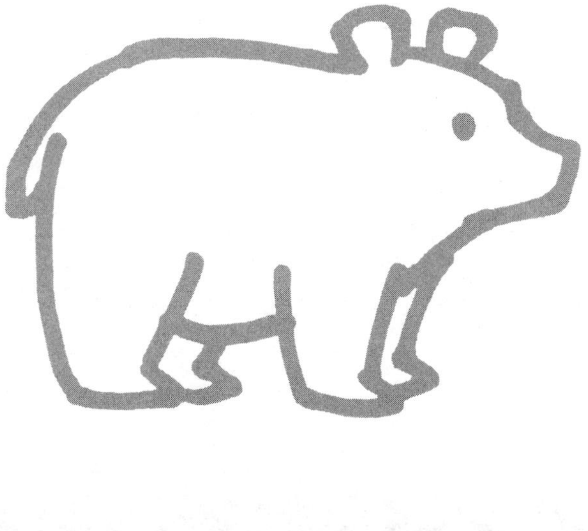

Are there any fish to catch?

Draw all the stars in the sky!

Carve something out of this log.

What can you make out of these logs?

Draw pine needles on the branches.

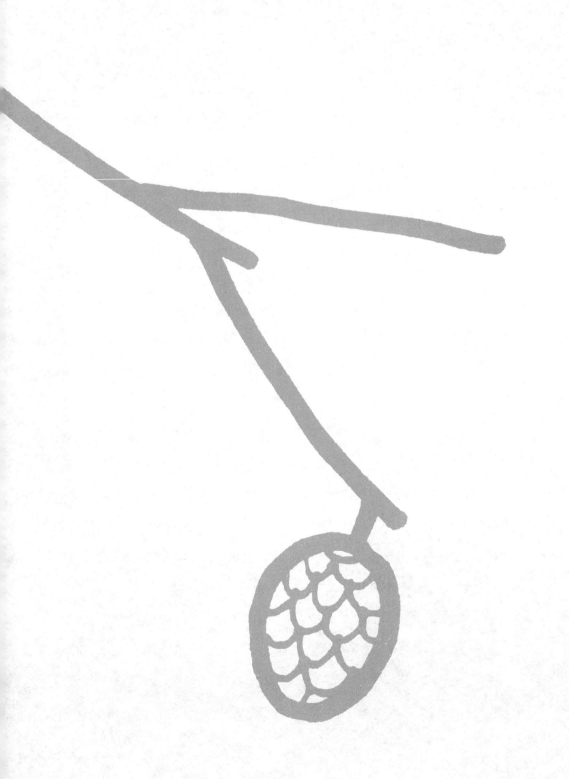

Who lives in the branches?

Load the truck with logs.

Color the hat.

Aleut hunting hat

Now make your own.

Draw a drum for the Unangan drummer.

THE INTERIOR

Draw the dogs pulling the dogsled.

What will you pack on your dogsled?

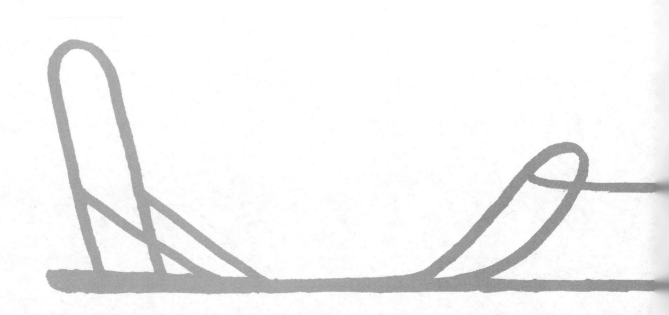

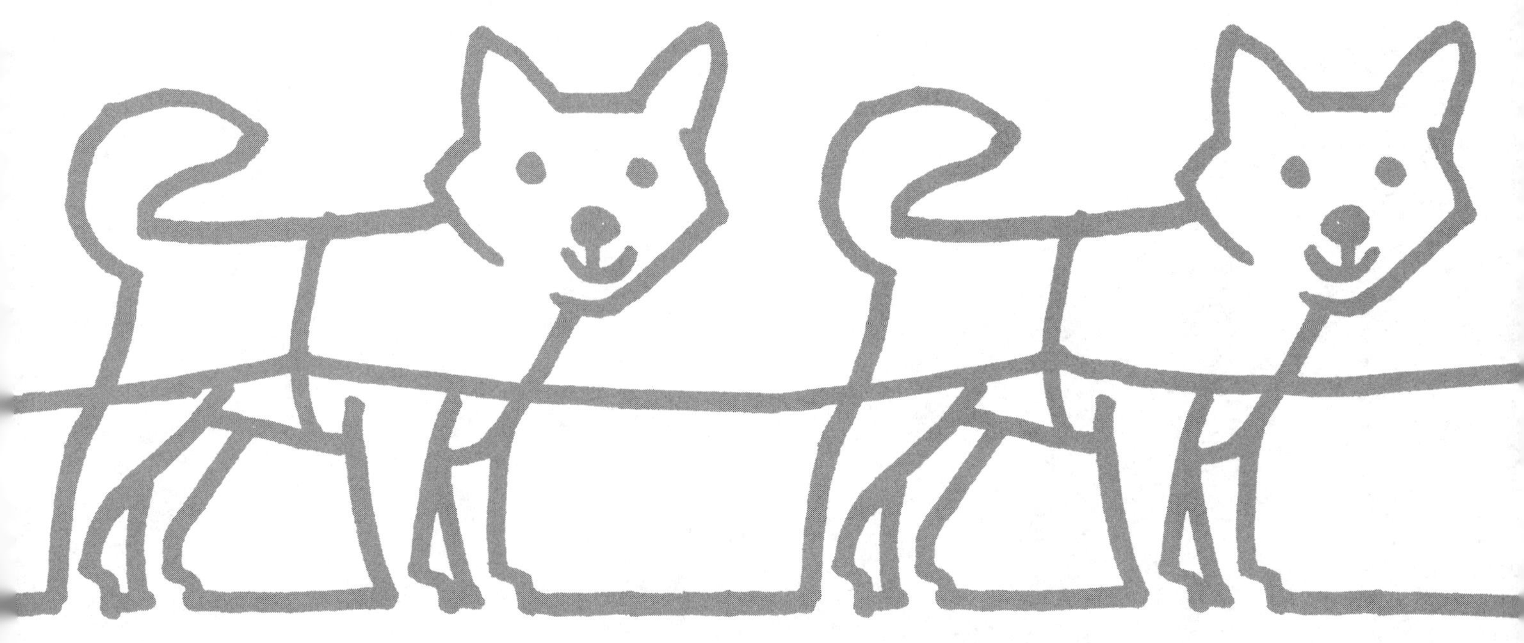

Now get your sled from Anchorage to Nome for the Iditarod Trail Sled Dog Race.

(If it's an even year, turn right at Ophir; if it's an odd year, turn left. Get back on the trail at Kaltag.)

Galena

Ruby

Cripple

(Even years)

Ophir

Takotna

Nikolai

McGrath

Rohn

Finger
Lake

Skwentna

Rainy
Pass

Willow

Campbell
Airstrip

Yentna

Anchorage

Connect the dots.

Danny and Debbie hear a
noise outside their tent.
What is it?

What's chasing them?

How long are the walrus's tusks?

Dall sheep live on steep cliffs.
How steep is this one?

Who is climbing Denali?

Find the words: caribou, Denali,
dogsled, Iditarod, moose.

```
S D O O D I P N
S E W E D A T
C L T N I L H
B S M A T S F
K G H L A T Z
U O B I R A C
V D E S O O M
C J J B D M I
```

Color the North Pole.

North Pole, Alaska

Is there any gold in the prospector's pan?

Draw a big gold nugget.

Draw antlers on the reindeer.

Draw lacings on the snowshoes.

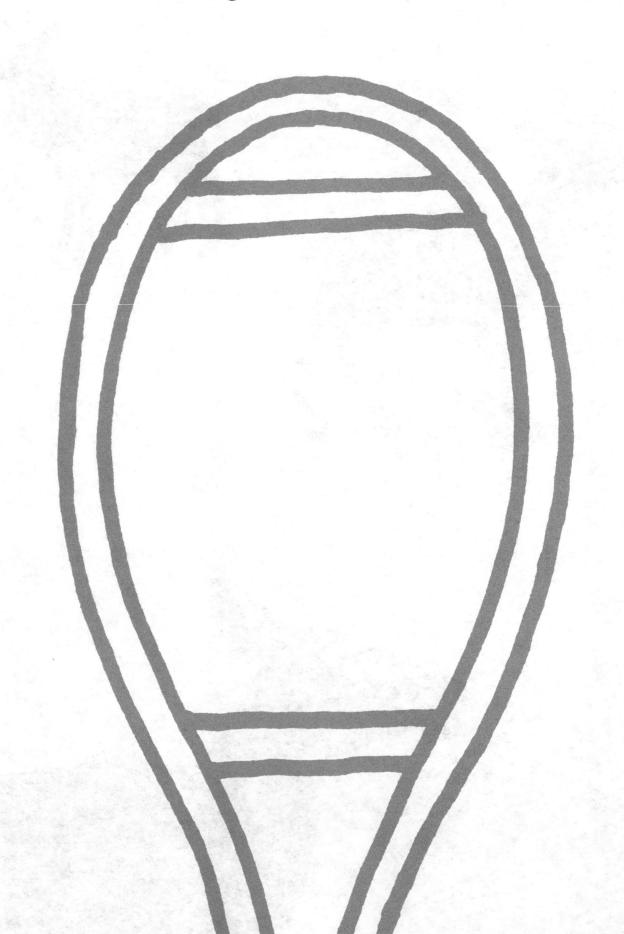

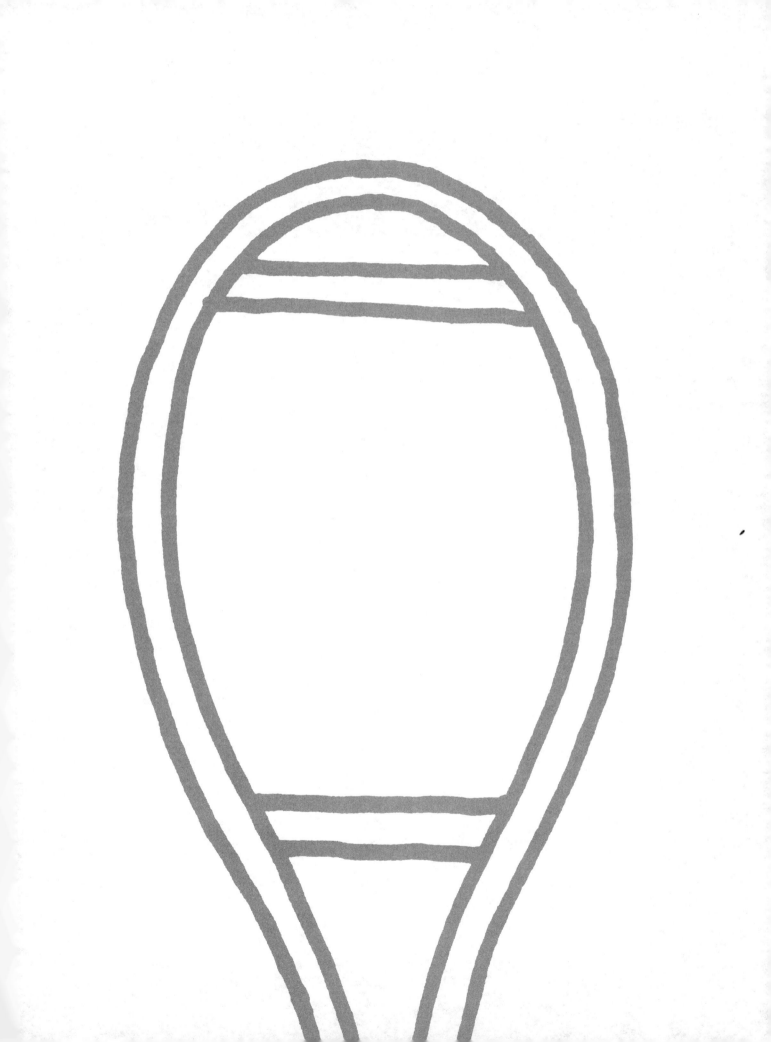

Carve the ice into ice sculptures.

World Ice Art Championships, Fairbanks

Color the winter clothes.

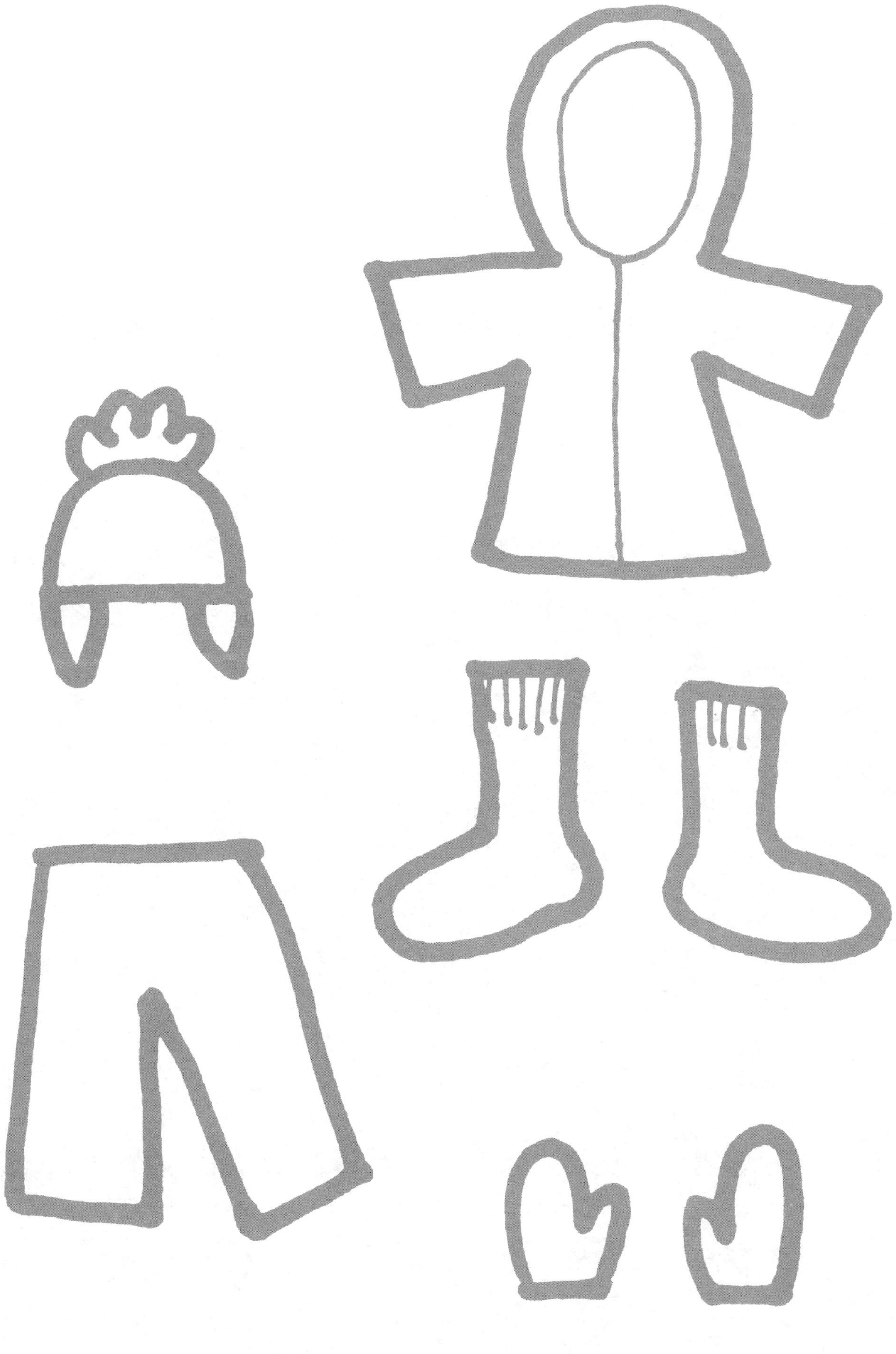

Draw a bridge for the train.

Draw your own train.

What animals are hiding in the forest?

Help Danny get
across the ice.

Color the mask.

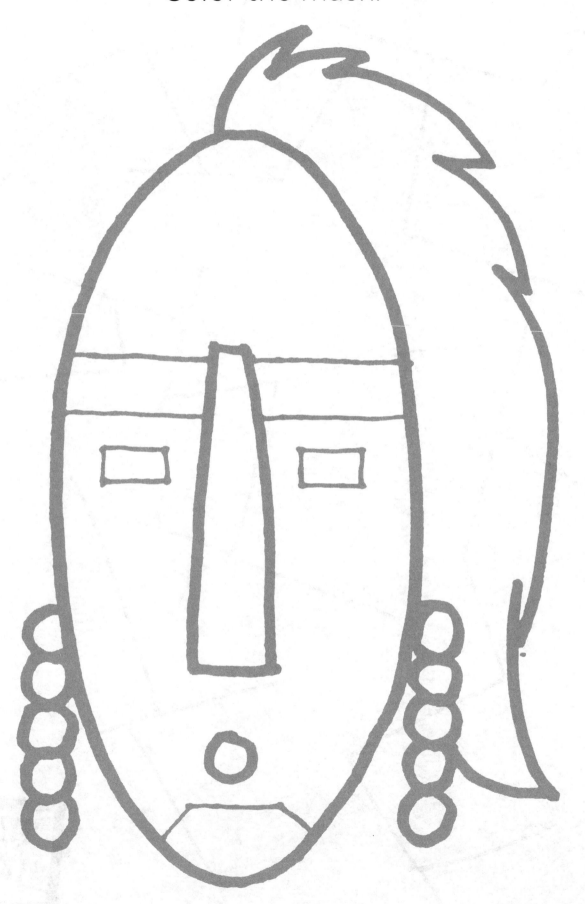

Athabascan mask

Now make your own.

Color the beaded mittens.

Athabascan moose-skin mittens

This is a polar bear in a snowstorm.
Draw the rest of the bear.

Color the Alaska flag.

Crossword

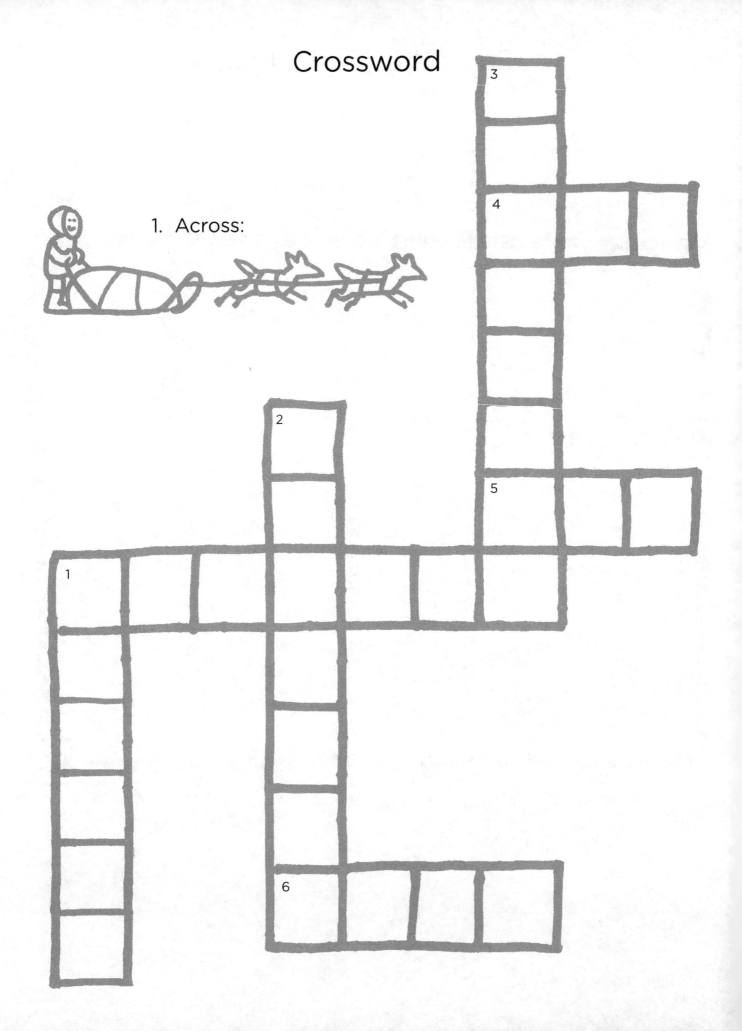

1. Across:

1. Down:
   The Great One

2. Down:

3. Down:
   The big dogsled race

4. Across:

5. Across:

6. Across:
   Eureka!

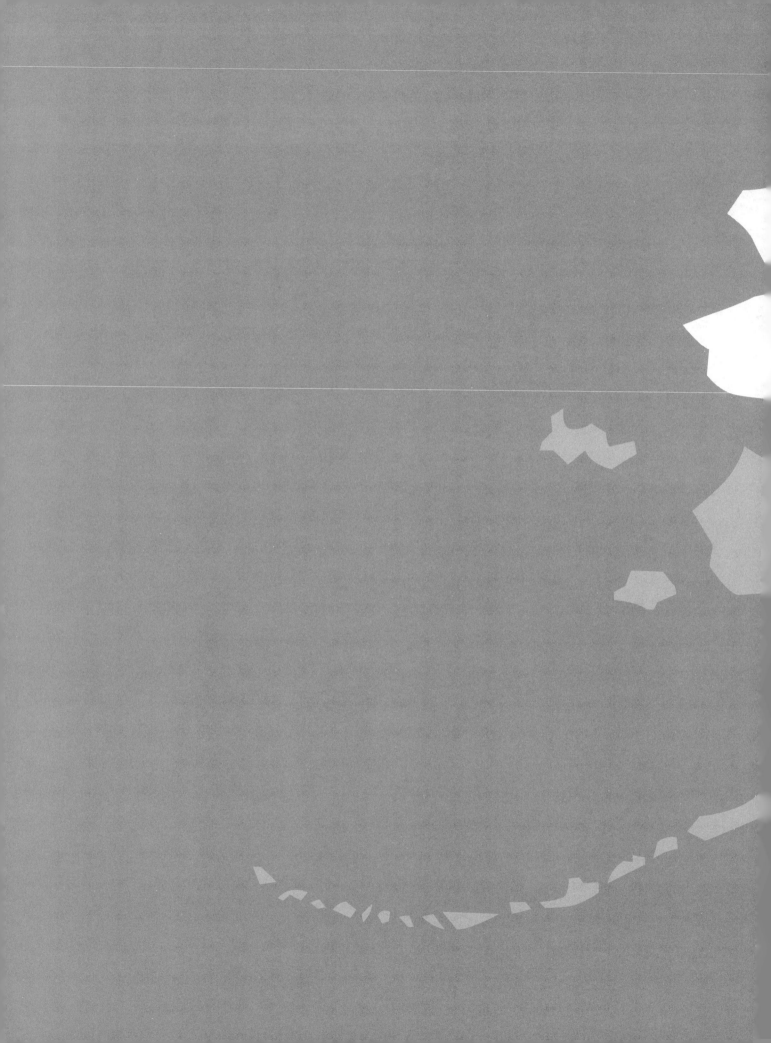

THE FAR NORTH

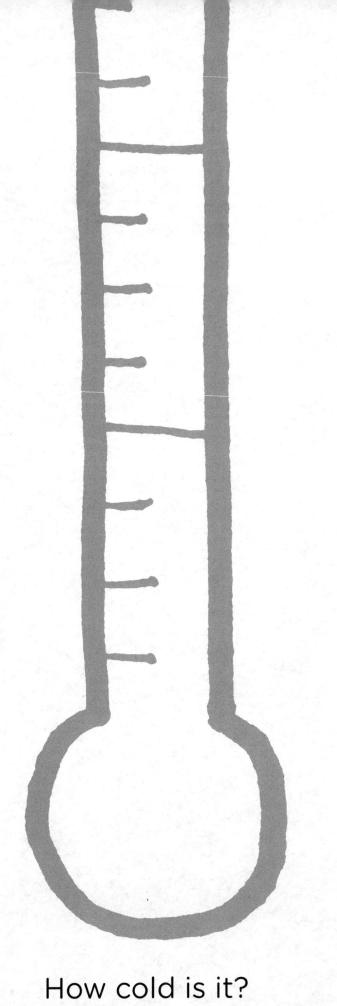

How cold is it?

Draw fur on the yak.

Draw the Northern Lights.

Color the mukluk.

Now draw your own.

Find the words: fishing, ice, mukluks,
Nome, plane, walrus.

```
S U R L A W X
E X J N C I W
F I S H I N G
E N O M E C E
D N I M I P E
M T A M N X M
S K U L K U M
Y M Z F P X Q
```

Outdoorsmen store their food in a cache so animals can't get it. What's in your cache?

Who is trying
to reach it?

The mosquito is trying
to get you!

Where are Debbie and Danny
walking in their snowshoes?

Draw a whale's tail
sticking out of the water.

Build an igloo.

Now decorate the inside of your igloo.

What's swimming under the ice?

This is a caribou.
Draw the rest of the herd.

Draw someone in the parka.

How much firewood can you chop?

Get your tub ready for the bathtub race!

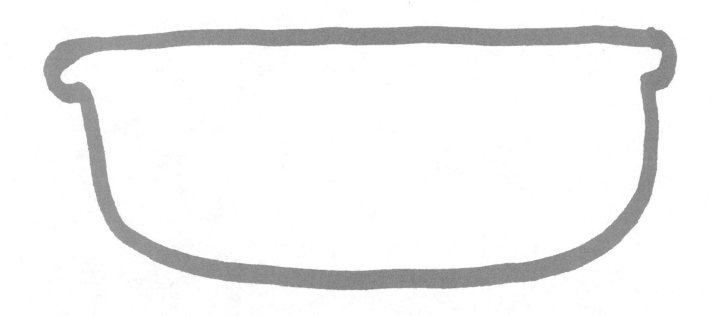

Who is floating on the ice?

Draw warm winter clothes for Danny and Debbie.

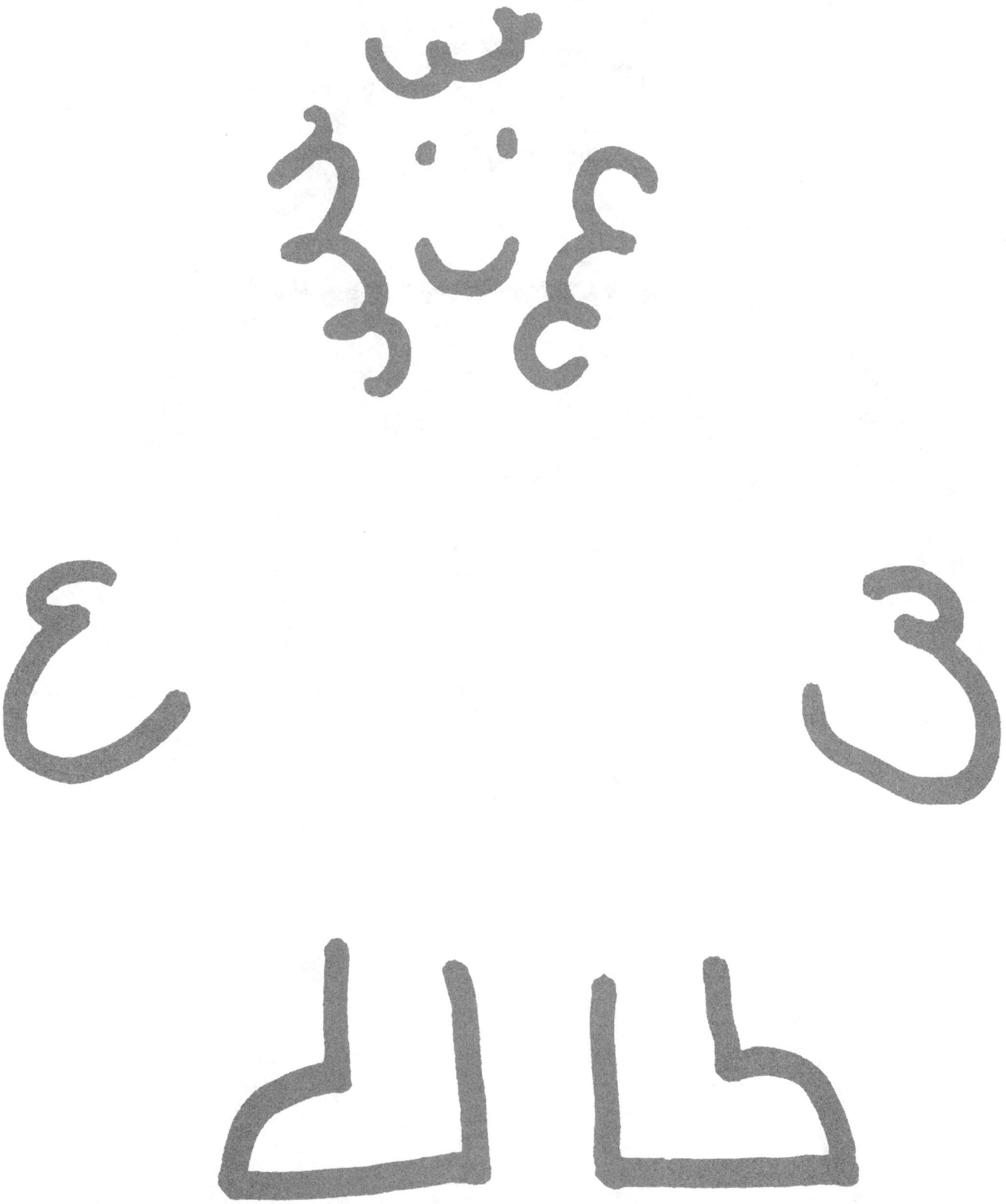

Draw a nice long scarf for Debbie.

Very long.

Draw winter hats for them.

Color their mittens!

Draw parkas on Danny and Debbie.

It's snowing! Fill the sky
with snowflakes.

What's under the snow?

How much snow is on the roof?

How long are the icicles?

Connect the dots on the caribou.

What does the hiker have in his pack?

Who is wearing skis?

Who is wearing snowshoes?

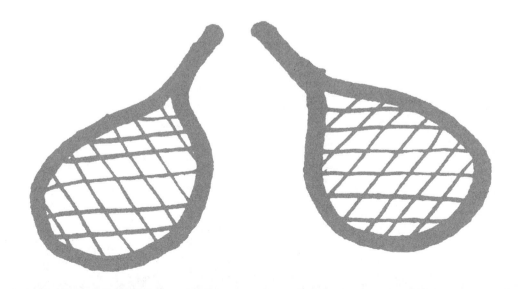

Draw something warm.

Draw something cold.

Draw a sunset.

What will you do when the
sun is out all night?

Color the mask.

Inupiaq mask